D1275849

Routes of Science

Medicine

Jen Green

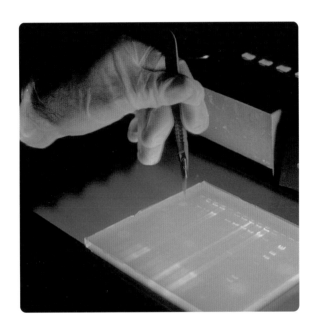

BLACKBIRCH®
PRESS

San Diego • Detroit • New York • San Francisco • Cleveland • New Haven, Conn. • Waterville, Maine • London • Munich

THOMSON

GALE

Every effort has been made to trace the
owners of copyrighted material.

PHOTOGRAPHIC CREDITS
Cover: University of Pennsylvania
Library/Smith Image Collection (l);
Science & Society Picture Library (t);
Dynamic Graphics (b).

AKG: Peter Conolly 17; **Herbert Kraft:** 6br;
Art Explosion: 6bl; **Corbis:** Gianni Dagli Orti
14bl, 15, Todd A. Gipstein 8; **Digital Vision:**
29; **Dynamic Graphics:** 34; **Getty Images:**
Hulton Archive 30r, 31; **Institute for
Traditional Medicine:** 11; **Mary Evans Picture
Library:** 10, 12, 18, 19t; **National Human
Genome Research Institute:** 4–5; **National
Library of Medicine:** 15, 16, 20l, 20r, 25, 27r;
NASA: 35, 36; **PHIL:** 1; **Photos12.com:** 30l;
Science & Society Picture Library: 7, 24l;
Topham Picturepoint: 9, 14c, 23t, 23b, 24c,
26, 29b, 32; **University of Pennsylvania:**
Smith Collection 19c, 19b, 21, 27l.

Consultant: Kathleen W. Jones, Ph.D.
  Medical historian,
  Department of History,
  Virginia Tech,
  Blacksburg, Virginia

For The Brown Reference Group plc
Text: Jen Green
Project Editor: Sydney Francis
Designer: Elizabeth Healey
Picture Researcher: Helen Simm
Illustrators: Darren Awuah,
  Richard Burgess, and Mark Walker
Managing Editor: Bridget Giles
Art Director: Dave Goodman
Children's Publisher: Anne O'Daly
Production Director: Alastair Gourlay
Editorial Director: Lindsey Lowe

LIBRARY OF CONGRESS CATALOGING-IN-PUBLICATION DATA

Green, Jen.
  Medicine / by Jen Green.
    p. cm. — (Routes of science)
  Includes bibliographical references and index.
  Contents: Ancient medicine — Eastern medicine — Greece and Rome — The Dark
Ages and the Renaissance — A scientific approach — Modern medicine.
    ISBN 1-4103-0168-0 (hardback : alk. paper)
  1. Medicine—History—Juvenile literature. 2. Medicine—Juvenile literature. [1.
Medicine—History. 2. Medical innovations.] I. Title. II. Series.

  R133.5.G74 2004
  610—dc22   2003012999

CONTENTS

INTRODUCTION

If a doctor from 1900 could be transported to the present, he or she would be amazed at the changes that have taken place in the last hundred years. Yet what has happened in the last century is just the latest chapter in a story that has been unfolding for three thousand years or more—the history of medicine.

ALL LIVING THINGS SUFFER FROM disease and injury, and eventually die. The aims of medicine are to ease suffering and to save people from untimely deaths. Modern medical care has three elements: diagnosis (identification of illness), treatment, and prevention. The body recovers naturally from some illnesses, but many need treatment. Treatment, or therapy, may take many forms, two of which are drugs (chemicals that can be used to treat illness) and surgery.

From prehistoric times to the Middle Ages, Western medicine was linked with magic and superstition. For centuries, people believed that disease was caused by witchcraft or represented punishment for sinful behavior. Early doctors were priests as well as healers. They used prayers and simple remedies to try to heal the sick. Ancient Greek and Roman doctors were the first to take a more rational approach, but they were held back by lack of scientific knowledge.

In the seventeenth century the development of scientific methods began to dispel many of the medical myths that had grown up in previous centuries. In the nineteenth century scientists discovered the link between germs and disease. Around the same time, surgeons began to use anesthesia to numb pain during operations, and to sterilize operating rooms. The twentieth century saw the first germ-killing antibiotics. These were all major steps in the history of medicine.

In developed countries doctors use drugs, surgery, and a range of equipment to cure, control, or prevent most illnesses. As a result, more people today live far longer than their ancestors. Modern medicine is very expensive, however, and poorer countries often cannot afford it.

Progress in medicine has not always been smooth, and medical science has taken some strange twists and turns. Yet in a hundred years' time, many medical techniques that are new today will seem old-fashioned. Medicine will have moved on.

1 ANCIENT MEDICINE

Medical practice dates back to Stone Age times, long before writing was invented. Later, Egyptian and Middle Eastern doctors developed more sophisticated techniques.

IN EARLY STONE AGE TIMES MORE than ten thousand years ago, people did not live in settled communities. They wandered from place to place, hunting wild animals and gathering plants for food. Gradually people learned that (**certain plants**) had healing properties and could be used as medicines. Before the invention of writing, this knowledge was passed on from generation to generation by word of mouth.

Plant Medicines

Plants have been used as medicines for up to fifty thousand years. People gradually discovered that certain herbs helped heal wounds and ease problems such as indigestion. Women may have specialized in this knowledge since they gathered plants for food. Plants are still used as a basis for many modern medicines. For example, foxglove (right) contains digitalis, a substance that is used today to treat heart disease.

Shamans

A shaman's job was to communicate with the spirits. Many shamans entered a trancelike state in which they asked the spirits for help. Cave paintings such as this one (below), which is from Ariege in France and is more than thirty thousand years old, suggest that some shamans wore animal skins when at work.

Trepanning

Trepanning was carried out in many parts of the world from around twenty thousand years ago. The technique involves cutting or drilling a hole in the skull with a knife or simple drill. Trepanning was probably carried out to cure headaches or release evil spirits. Signs of healing around the holes in trepanned skulls suggest that many people survived one or even several of these operations.

A trepanned skull from c. *2200–2000* B.C.

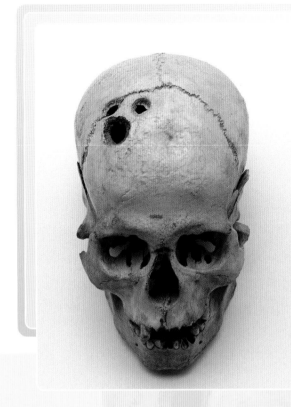

For Stone Age people, life was hard and often short. Most men lived to only about thirty-five years old. Most women lived to only about thirty, because of the extra strains of bearing children. People believed that gods or evil spirits caused illness. **Shamans** (also called witch doctors or medicine men) prayed to the spirits on behalf of ordinary people. The relatives of sick people paid shamans to work cures.

The first operations were performed in Stone Age times using simple flint or bone tools. **Trepanning,** a form of surgery on the skull, was one of the earliest techniques. Ancient people also reset broken bones.

Around 7000 B.C., people began to settle in one place and farm the land.

The Code of Hammurabi

The Code of Hammurabi is a set of laws that covered life in ancient Mesopotamia. It dates from around 1770 B.C. Seventeen of the 282 laws relate to medicine. The code sets out the rewards surgeons would receive for performing successful operations on people of various ranks: ten silver shekels for a saving the life of a nobleman, five for a commoner, and two for a slave. Details of severe punishments for unsuccessful operations were also given: "If a physician performed an operation and caused a lord's death . . . they shall cut off his hand."

This replica stone tablet is a Mesopotamian medical prescription.

First, villages and then cities grew up, but settled life brought increased risk of infection because many people lived close together in conditions that would be considered unsanitary today. New medical practices emerged to tackle this problem.

One of the first centers of civilization was the ancient land of Mesopotamia in what is now Iraq. The Mesopotamians used a combination of magic, astronomy, herbs, and simple surgery to treat illness. They lanced boils, washed wounds, and made ointments and bandages. When the Mesopotamians invented writing around 3300 B.C., medical techniques were recorded for the first time. The **Code of Hammurabi** is one such text.

In ancient Egypt, three branches of medicine had developed by around 2000 B.C. People used spells to ward off evil spirits, and prayed to Imhotep, the god of healing. They also, however, employed surgeons to carry out simple operations, and physicians to supply medicines. The Egyptians probably gained some knowledge of anatomy (the structure of the body) through the technique of mummification, which they used to preserve the bodies of their dead.

The Jewish people of ancient Palestine developed a knowledge of medicine by around 1200 B.C. They practiced first aid and were among the first to understand the importance of sanitation to prevent disease from spreading.

Imhotep, God of Healing

Imhotep, an Egyptian nobleman who lived around 2650 B.C., is the world's first physician whose name is known. He was chief advisor to a pharaoh named King Djoser. A doctor and an administrator, Imhotep was also a priest, an astronomer, and a gifted architect who built one of the first pyramids. After his death he was worshiped as a god, and his tomb became a temple of healing.

Fragment of an ancient Egyptian wall engraving of Imhotep (far right), surgical instruments (center), and birthing chairs (left).

Jewish Medicine

In ancient times, Jewish people with contagious diseases were isolated in an early form of quarantine. Their homes were later disinfected. Water was kept as clean as possible, and the eating of pork and other foods that might carry disease was forbidden.

2 EASTERN MEDICINE

In ancient times, civilization flourished in the East, in India and China. Early Indian and Chinese doctors developed branches of medicine that are still widely used today.

IN CHINA, CIVILIZATION DATES back more than five thousand years. Chinese medicine developed from about 2000 B.C. to A.D. 500. Its basic assumptions have changed little since then. This medicine is based on the belief that two basic forces, called **yin and yang,** flow through the human body. Illness results when the two become unbalanced. To restore the balance, Chinese doctors developed the practice of **acupuncture**.

Yin and Yang

In Chinese philosophy, yang is all things that are bright, warm, dry, active, and male. Yin is the opposite: dark, cool, moist, passive, and female. Sickness results if the forces are unbalanced; for example, if a person spends too much time being active and gets too little rest. A change of diet, exercise, herbal remedies, and acupuncture could all help restore the balance.

A Chinese philosopher carrying the yin-yang symbol in his left hand.

What is Acupuncture?

In China, acupuncture has been used for at least three thousand years to relieve pain and sickness. Acupuncture involves puncturing the skin with fine needles at key points in the body. Alternatively, a small cone containing crushed herbs is placed on the acupuncture point, and the herbs burned, a practice called moxibustion. Both practices are thought to free the flow of energy (*chi* in Chinese) along twelve pathways in the body called meridians. In China, major operations are at times carried out using only acupuncture to numb the pain.

Acupuncture points are linked by channels called meridians.

Hua T'o

The surgeon Hua T'o lived about A.D. 115–205. One of his patients was a general named Kuan Yun. When a poisoned arrow hit Kuan Yun, Hua T'o scraped out the wound while the general drank wine and played board games. Later, Hua T'o made the mistake of treating Kuan Yun's enemy, Tsao Tsao. Hua

A twentieth-century painting of Hua T'o.

T'o was beginning treatment when Tsao became suspicious that the surgeon was about to harm him. Tsao had Hua T'o executed on the spot.

Acupuncture is still widely practiced in Asian countries, and some modern Western doctors have begun to adopt acupuncture to treat pain.

Medicine became a profession in China by A.D. 500. Students had to pass a series of examinations to qualify as doctors. Surgery was rare. Surgeons were generally looked down on as "third-class graduates," but the name of one famous surgeon, Hua T'o, has passed into history.

The *Nei Ching*

An early medical textbook, the *Nei Ching* was written some time between 450 and 300 B.C. It is mainly about acupuncture. It takes the form of a conversation between the legendary Yellow Emperor, Huang Ti (left), who is said to have lived around 2600 B.C., and his chief minister. According to legend, Huang Ti ruled China for a hundred years and then rose to heaven on a dragon.

The Three Humors

According to Ayurvedic philosophy, three major substances—air, bile, and phlegm—make up the tissues of the body. This idea is similar to the Greek notion of the four humors (*see* page 15).

Chinese doctors used hundreds of remedies made from herbs and sometimes animals to cure different ailments. Thousands of years ago, they prescribed the use of the horsetail plant to relieve breathing problems. In the 1920s, western doctors began to use ephedrine, an extract from the same plant, to help asthma sufferers. After writing was invented in China around 1500 B.C., remedies were recorded. The **Nei Ching** was an important medical textbook.

In India, traditional medicine is known as **ayurveda,** a word that means "recipe for long life." Ayurveda was developed between 2400 B.C. and A.D. 500. Like Chinese medicine, its basic concepts have changed little since then. This system of thought is linked to Hinduism, one of India's main faiths. One key idea was that the body's

Chakras

The seven chakras (right) lie along the line of the spine. Each is linked to important glands and organs. Sickness is believed to result if the chakras become unbalanced. Doctors might restore balance by giving herbal remedies or massages, by prescribing the practice of yoga, or by uttering sacred chants.

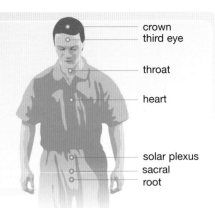

crown
third eye
throat
heart
solar plexus
sacral
root

energy flowed along channels called **chakras.** This is similar to the idea of meridians in Chinese philosophy. A total of 107 key points in the body, or *marmas*, are vital to health. Some of these points are located on major arteries, nerves, or muscles.

As in China, Indian doctors used hundreds of remedies to treat sickness. These were made from plants, animals, or minerals such as gold, silver, or iron. Indian doctors excelled at surgery. They performed a variety of both internal and external operations. Doctors sewed up wounds, treated eye cataracts (in which the lens becomes cloudy), and removed kidney and bladder stones. They also performed **plastic surgery.** Indian surgeons used the jaws of black ants, which oozed an antiseptic (germ-killing) poison, instead of sutures (stitches) to close wounds.

Plastic Surgery in Ancient India

Operations performed by Indian doctors included plastic surgery to restore ears and noses—parts that were sometimes cut off to punish criminals. To restore the nose, the surgeon cut a flap of skin from the forehead and brought it down to cover the nose. The air passages were kept open by inserting wooden tubes to form the nostrils. The modern operation of rhinoplasty (nose surgery) is based on a similar technique.

3 GREECE AND ROME

The origins of Western medicine can be traced back to the ancient Greek and Roman civilizations. The doctors Hippocrates and Galen were major figures of their time.

GREEK CIVILIZATION FLOURISHED from about 800 B.C. to 150 B.C. In the early days, healing was linked with supernatural forces, especially with (**Asclepius,**) the god of healing. Later the great physician (**Hippocrates**) separated medicine from superstition. Hippocrates also devised a code of conduct for doctors called the (**Hippocratic oath.**)

Asclepius, God of Healing

In ancient Greece many people prayed to the god Asclepius to cure them from illness. Sick people would spend the night in Asclepius's temple. If they were lucky, the god would visit them in a dream to give medical advice. Asclepius's daughters Hygeia, goddess of health, and Panacea, goddess of healing, are remembered in the words "hygiene" and "panacea" ("panacea" means a cure for all illness). Both men and women trained as doctors in ancient Greece.

Greek carving from the fourth century B.C. of Asclepius treating a patient.

Hippocrates

Hippocrates (c. 460–370 B.C.; right) came from the Greek island of Kos and founded a medical school there. "Every disease has its own nature, and arises from natural causes," he wrote. He pioneered the art of diagnosis, and recommended that doctors consider their patients' symptoms and case histories carefully before identifying illnesses. Then, he said, they should make a prognosis—a prediction of the outcome—before giving treatment, and keep a record of what happened. Doctors still follow this procedure today.

Around 300 B.C. the Greek city of Alexandria in Egypt became a center of learning and medicine. For a time, doctors there were allowed to dissect human corpses, to find out about the body's structure. The Alexandrian doctor Herophilus (c. 335–280 B.C.) founded the science of anatomy (the study of the human body).

Like Chinese and Indian doctors, the Greeks believed that balance in the body was vital to health. They stressed the importance of maintaining balance between four fluids in the body called the **four humors.**

The Hippocratic Oath

In swearing the Hippocratic oath, doctors vowed to serve the sick and not misuse their skills: "I will prescribe treatment to the best of my ability for the good of the sick, and never for a harmful purpose." The oath required doctors to be discreet and keep any secrets revealed to them through their work. Some doctors still swear a version of this oath.

A version of the Hippocratic oath. The oath is still used by doctors today.

The Four Humors

The ancient Greeks believed that the universe was made of four elements: air, water, fire, and earth. Similarly, the human body was made up of four humors (fluids): blood, phlegm, yellow bile, and black bile. Imbalances were corrected by releasing the excess fluid or "vicious humor." Treatments included bleeding patients by cutting into a vein or applying bloodsucking leeches, and giving herbs to cause diarrhea or vomiting.

Galen

Physician Claudius Galen (*c.* A.D. 130–200) was born in the Greek city of Pergamum, now in Turkey. He gained some knowledge of anatomy by operating on wounded gladiators. Then he traveled to Rome and impressed everyone by dissecting animals such as pigs. (The Romans had made it illegal to dissect humans.) Galen became rich and famous, but his arrogant and rude manner made him generally unpopular. Galen wrote more than one hundred books. His works became a major authority for the next twelve hundred years, but many of his ideas and methods were later challenged.

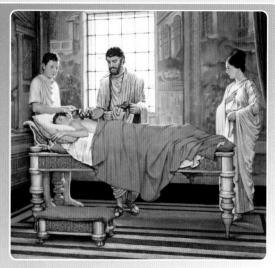

Galen treating a patient using the technique of cupping (see page 17).

Around 250 B.C., the Romans conquered Greece. They gradually established a huge empire that covered most of Europe, North Africa, and western Asia, and lasted until the fifth century A.D. The Romans used the medical knowledge of Greece and Egypt and imported Greek doctors. In Rome, as in Greece, women as well as men could train as doctors. Women tended to specialize in female health problems. Doctors might work independently, or be employed by a rich family, or even by a town to look after its citizens. A Greek physician named Claudius Galen was the most famous doctor of Roman times.

The Romans were pioneers in the area of public health, both in everyday life and in the military. They built

Military Medicine

The Roman Empire needed a huge army to maintain law and order. Hygiene was vital to prevent disease from spreading through the ranks. Forts were supplied with clean water and sanitation. They were built in healthful places, away from swamps infested by mosquitoes that carried the deadly disease malaria. The first hospitals were set up to treat soldiers injured on the battlefield.

A reconstruction of the third-century A.D. latrine in the Roman fort of Housesteads on Hadrian's Wall in northern England.

Cupping

This technique involved placing a cup that contained burning cloth over the skin or an open wound to draw out poisonous fluid. As the cloth burned, it used up the oxygen in the cup, thereby creating a vacuum (empty space) that drew out blood or pus. Cupping was carried out to restore the balance of the four humors.

graceful aqueducts to bring freshwater supplies to cities, and sewage systems to dispose of waste. They also built public baths and latrines, or toilets. Bathing and even going to the toilet were social activities, with separate facilities for men and women.

The Romans were also expert craftsmen, who made fine tools such as probes and scalpels to perform examinations and operations. Common procedures included (cupping) to remove poison from the body. The Romans were also skilled at using herbal remedies.

4 THE DARK AGES AND THE RENAISSANCE

After the Roman Empire broke up, classical learning developed by the Greeks and Romans was mostly forgotten in the West. European medicine did not move forward again until the fourteenth century.

IN THE FIFTH CENTURY A.D. Rome fell to invading tribes from the north, and the Dark Ages began. In Europe, little progress was made in science for almost a thousand years. Superstition flourished. Illness was seen as a punishment from God, and people prayed to their favorite saint

Women Healers

During medieval times, women were not allowed to train as doctors, though they could still be midwives and give herbal remedies. In some areas female healers were persecuted as witches; they were tortured and burned at the stake. Before, female physicians or "wise women" had helped keep communities healthy, but this was no longer possible.

A female physician uses herbs to heal a sick child.

The Plague

The Black Death, or bubonic plague, was a severe epidemic that wiped out more than 70 million people, about a quarter of Europe's population, in the 1340s. The plague was caused by bacteria that lived inside fleas that lived on rats. At the time no one knew this, and people thought God had sent the plague to punish them for being sinful. Groups called flagellants (right) wandered the country whipping themselves to try to gain forgiveness for their sins.

for healing. **Women healers** were discouraged, and hospitals were run by religious orders rather than trained doctors. This was encouraged by the Christian religion.

Only the concept of the four humors survived from Greek and Roman learning. Bloodletting and purging, to rid the body of poisonous fluids, were used for all sorts of illnesses. Doctors mainly diagnosed patients by studying their urine, a technique called uroscopy. When the **bubonic plague** struck Europe in the 1340s, people saw it as a divine punishment for sins, rather than an infectious disease.

In contrast, learning flourished in **Arab countries**. Muslim scholars translated Greek and Roman texts

Arab Doctors

Rhazes (Al Rhasi, 850–932) was a chief physician of Baghdad during the tenth century. He was the first to distinguish between the diseases measles and smallpox. The Persian doctor Avicenna (Ibn Sina, 980–1037; right) wrote a huge medical encyclopedia called the *Canon of Medicine*. It summed up the medical knowledge of the time and remained important for the next six hundred years.

AVICENNA
ex codice antiquo Galeni.

19

into Arabic and added their own discoveries. This kept alive the learning of the ancient Greeks. In the seventh century, Muslim religion and culture spread through the Middle East, North Africa, and Spain. Medical schools were set up in Baghdad (now in Iraq); in Cairo, Egypt; and in Cordoba, Spain. Rhazes and Avicenna were two important Arab doctors.

In the late fourteenth century the Renaissance saw the beginning of a new interest in science in Europe. (The word *renaissance* means "rebirth.") This movement began in Italy, where the first medical schools had been

Ambroise Paré, Barber-surgeon

During medieval times, surgeons were generally looked down on. Barber-surgeons often carried out operations. They also cut people's hair. In the sixteenth century, Ambroise Paré (1510–1590; above) trained as a barber-surgeon and then became an army doctor. He learned through experience to dress wounds with clean bandages instead of cauterizing them (sealing them with boiling oil) as was usual. Paré eventually became surgeon to the French king. When other doctors criticized him because of his lack of formal training, he wrote an autobiography in which he described many of his new techniques.

Andreas Vesalius

Andreas Vesalius (1514–1564; right) was a Belgian doctor who became professor of anatomy at the University of Padua in Italy. He made many discoveries about anatomy, which he described in his book *On the Structure of the Human Body* (1543). Before this, the great Italian artist and inventor Leonardo da Vinci (1452–1519) had also performed dissections in secret and made many beautiful drawings, but his work remained hidden for hundreds of years.

founded several centuries earlier, and quickly spread to the rest of Europe. Scholars translated Greek and Roman works back from the Arabic and revived classical learning.

Before the Renaissance the dissection of human corpses was not allowed, so no one could learn about anatomy. Dissection again became legal, and in Italy, **Andreas Vesalius** produced the first accurate textbook on anatomy, which soon replaced Galen's works. In France, an army surgeon named **Ambroise Paré** pioneered so many new surgical techniques that he is called "the father of modern surgery." The Swiss physician **Philippus Paracelsus** experimented with chemicals to create effective new drugs.

The lively portraiture of y most famous and profound Philosopher & Physitian Aureolus Philippus Theophrastus Paracelsus Bombast, of Hohenneim who was poysned the 47 yeare of his age.
Are to be sould by Willia Webb at y Globe. Io.Payne foul

Philippus Paracelsus

Paracelsus (1493–1541; left) was a Swiss physician. An open-minded man, he rejected much of the established learning about medicine. Appointed lecturer at the University of Basle, Switzerland, he began his lectures by throwing the works of Galen and Avicenna on a bonfire. He declared: "Reading never made a doctor. Patients are the only books." Paracelsus was ahead of his time in many ways. He stressed the body's natural ability to heal itself, and also pioneered the use of minerals such as sulfur, iron, and mercury in the manufacture of drugs.

5 A SCIENTIFIC APPROACH

The period between 1600 and 1900 was a vital time in the history of Western medicine. Many important discoveries were made, but old-fashioned practices such as bloodletting still continued.

IN THE 1620S ENGLISH PHYSICIAN William Harvey discovered that blood (circulated) throughout the body. Harvey also realized that the heart worked as a pump.

Around 1600 the invention of the (microscope) revealed tiny worlds invisible to the naked eye. During the mid-1600s, Antoni van Leeuwenhoek used microscopes to study the tiny

Blood Circulation

English physician William Harvey (1578–1657) dissected humans and other animals to find out about blood circulation. Greek and Roman doctors understood that blood moved, but not how it circulated. Harvey's breakthrough was important because it showed that the body worked in ways that were related to its structure. This encouraged scientists to find out more about anatomy.

Oxygen-poor blood (blue) is pumped by the heart to the lungs to pick up oxygen. Oxygen-rich blood (red) travels back to the heart, which pumps it around the body. Body cells need oxygen to stay alive.

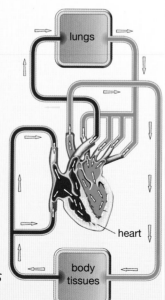

lungs

heart

body tissues

Under the Microscope

Dutch scientist Antoni van Leeuwenhoek (1632–1723) spent his free time making microscopes and studying the small worlds they revealed. Under the microscope he saw sperm, muscle fibers, and minute living things he called "animalcules" or "little animals." These turned out to be bacteria and other microorganisms. He also studied red blood cells and noted that humans, fish, and frogs had blood cells of different shapes.

Vaccination

Country doctor Edward Jenner (1749–1823) noticed that local milkmaids who caught the disease cowpox from their animals never developed smallpox. He concluded that overcoming cowpox made people naturally immune to smallpox. In a risky

experiment, he prepared a vaccine from cowpox sores, and administered it to a young boy (left). When he injected the same patient with smallpox afterward, the disease did not develop. The experiment worked. The word vaccine comes from the Latin word *vacca*, meaning "cow."

organisms we now call germs. No one, however, understood at the time that germs caused disease.

In 1796 English doctor Edward Jenner pioneered the process of **vaccination,** which stimulates the body's natural immune system to protect against disease. Jenner discovered a safe way to make people immune from the deadly disease

smallpox by giving them cowpox, a related but much less serious disease.

Later, German scientist Rudolf Virchow (1821–1902) made important discoveries about deadly diseases such as tuberculosis and cholera. Virchow studied the cells of diseased tissues to understand how disease develops. This was the beginning of pathology, the medical study of disease.

New Steps in Diagnosis

Inventions that aided diagnosis in the nineteenth century included the spirometer (left), an instrument to test a patient's lung capacity. This device helped doctors diagnose lung problems. By the late 1800s doctors were using stopwatches to time their patients' pulses, and taking temperatures using thermometers (originally invented in the sixteenth century by the astronomer Galileo Galilei.) Also in the late 1800s, doctors began to measure blood pressure using a machine called a sphygmomanometer, and examine eyes using an ophthalmoscope.

A Woman Doctor

Scottish doctor James (Miranda) Barry (died 1865; left) trained at Edinburgh Medical School in the early 1800s and afterward practiced medicine for more than fifty years. Barry became Inspector General of Hospitals and was renowned for being both quick-tempered and a crack shot with a pistol. When Barry died in 1865, he was found to have really been a woman.

In the nineteenth century, many new instruments were invented to help doctors (diagnose illness.) In 1816, French doctor René Laennec (1781–1826) invented the stethoscope, which allows doctors to listen to sounds inside the body and identify problems such as lung complaints.

As medicine became increasingly professional, women's role as healers dwindled. In Britain women were forbidden to train as doctors, so the only way a woman could practice medicine was by pretending to be a man. This occurred in the case of a Scottish doctor named (James Barry.) As men took over the care of women patients, they introduced new practices that suited doctors but not always their patients. For example, the practice of making women lie down during childbirth made a doctor's job easier, but did not help the birth. Even so, this practice survives to this day.

The 1840s saw a major new step in surgery—the development of anesthetics to relieve pain. Before this, patients who underwent surgery were given large quantities of alcohol or another drug to numb the pain.

Then they were held down by force. If they were lucky, they fainted. Around 1800, British scientists Humphry Davy (1778–1829) and Michael Faraday (1791–1867) discovered that both nitrous oxide (laughing gas) and ether dulled pain. American doctors Crawford Long and William Morton pioneered the practice of using ether as an anesthetic.

Anesthetics

In 1842, American surgeon Crawford Long (1815–1878) used ether to numb a patient while he removed a growth from the patient's neck. In 1846, dentist and medical student William Morton (1819–1868) administered ether during an operation at Boston Hospital (right). Morton went on to become one of the first professional anesthetists.

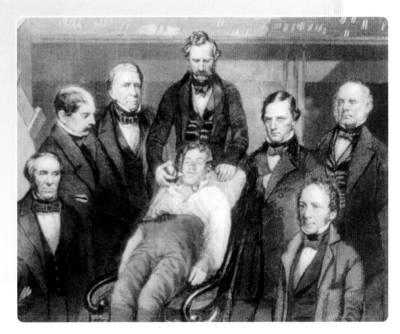

After the mid-1850s standards of nursing improved due to the work of nurse (**Florence Nightingale**) during the Crimean War (1853–1856). Until the mid-nineteenth century, no woman could train in a medical school in either Europe or North America. An American, Elizabeth Blackwell (1821–1910), was first to qualify as a doctor, followed by Englishwoman Elizabeth Garrett Anderson (1836–1917).

In the 1800s, French chemist (**Louis Pasteur**) made an important discovery when he linked disease with the microorganisms seen by Antoni van Leeuwenhoek in the 1600s. Pasteur and German chemist Robert Koch (1843–1910) discovered that bacteria caused a range of illnesses. After Pasteur showed that killing microorganisms stopped the spread of disease, standards of hygiene improved. Before this,

Florence Nightingale

English nurse Florence Nightingale (1820–1910) came from a well-to-do family. She resolved to become a nurse at a time when nursing was not seen as an acceptable career for a middle-class lady. In 1854 Nightingale took a team of nurses to the Crimea to care for wounded British soldiers (right). There she revolutionized nursing practice. On returning to Britain, she opened a training college for nurses in London. Nightingale Schools later opened in the United States, Canada, Australia, and Scandinavia.

The Work of Pasteur

Louis Pasteur (1822–1895; below) proved that bacteria cause decay and disease. He discovered that microorganisms cause wine and beer to ferment (brew) and invented the technique of pasteurization, which involves heating and then quickly cooling foods to kill bacteria. The germ theory of disease put to rest the Greek doctrine of the four humors. Pasteur also developed vaccines for the deadly diseases anthrax and rabies.

Lister and Antiseptics

British surgeon Joseph Lister (1827–1912; right) began to sterilize wounds by washing them with carbolic acid. Later, he invented a carbolic spray to kill germs during operations. People were doubtful about the value of Lister's work until the surgeon used his spray while he operated successfully on the British queen Victoria. Lister was eventually credited with having "saved more lives than all the wars of history have thrown away."

hospitals had paid little attention to cleanliness. Operating rooms were often dirty, and surgeons worked in bloodstained clothes. As a result, around half of all surgical patients died of infection.

English surgeon (Joseph Lister) pioneered the practice of working in antiseptic (bacteria-killing) conditions, after he learned of Pasteur's work.

Lister sprayed carbolic acid onto the site of operations to sterilize wounds. Later surgeons operated in aseptic, or germ-free, conditions by washing thoroughly, wearing surgical masks and gowns, and using steam-sterilized instruments. When sterilization became commonplace, the number of patients who died of infection after surgery dropped dramatically.

ROUTES OF SCIENCE · MEDICINE

6 MODERN MEDICINE

The twentieth century brought progress in many branches of medicine, including diagnosis and the development of drugs to fight disease and infection. Surgery also progressed, particularly after World War II.

IN 1895 GERMAN PHYSICIST Wilhelm Roentgen (1845–1923) discovered (**X rays.**) This allowed doctors to see inside the human body for the first time. Around 1900 the French physicists Pierre (1859–1906) and his wife Marie Curie (1867–1934) discovered the radioactive element radium. This was used in radiotherapy to treat cancer patients. About the same

X rays

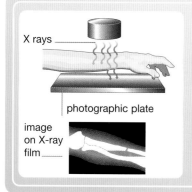

X rays

photographic plate

image on X-ray film

In 1895 Willem Roentgen discovered that a type of radiation he called X rays passed through soft body tissues but not bones or metal, and affected photographic film. He used the technique to photograph his wife's hand. X rays were soon used to detect broken bones, bullets embedded in patients' bodies, and metal objects such as coins that had been swallowed accidentally.

Blood Groups

After William Harvey's discovery of blood circulation in the seventeenth century, doctors had tried to transfuse (transfer) blood between humans, but these experiments had not worked. In 1900 scientist Karl Landsteiner (1868–1943) found out why when he discovered that there were several human blood groups that did not mix. This discovery paved the way for successful blood transfusions.

There are four main blood groups: O, A, B, and AB. The majority of the population—45%—is type O, 42% type A, 10% type B, and 3% type AB. Each group is then split into positive or negative types.

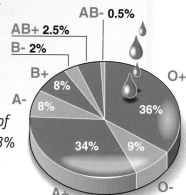

AB- 0.5%
AB+ 2.5%
B- 2%
B+ 8%
A- 8%
O+ 36%
34%
9%
A+
O-

Wonder Drug

Aspirin (right) has proved to be one of the most successful drugs ever. It is used to relieve pain, reduce fever, and thin the blood. In the 1820s scientists had discovered that salicylic acid, from willow bark, was a painkiller, but it irritated the stomach lining. By 1900 German chemist Felix Hoffmann (1868–1946) succeeded in manufacturing a similar chemical, called aspirin, which lessened the side effect to safer levels.

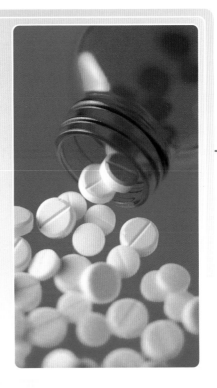

time, Austro-American scientist Karl Landsteiner discovered (**blood groups**.

In 1903 Dutch scientist Willem Einthoven (1860–1927) produced the first electrocardiograph (ECG), which showed electrical activity in the heart, using a machine called a galvanometer. Later, in the 1940s, the same technology was used to make the first electroencephalographs (EEGs), which measure brain activity. This allowed doctors to detect brain injuries and illnesses such as epilepsy.

In the twentieth century, many new drugs were developed. Some came from natural sources such as animals, plants, and fungi. Others were made synthetically. Around 1900, the wonder drug (**aspirin**) began to be produced.

The First Magic Bullet

Paul Ehrlich (1854–1915; left) and his Japanese assistant Sahachiro Hata (1872–1938) tested more than six hundred chemicals before they discovered one that worked on syphilis, a bacterial disease spread by sexual contact. They called the drug Salvarsan 606 because it was the 606th chemical they tested.

The Discovery of Penicillin

In 1928 Scottish scientist Alexander Fleming (1881–1955; right) was conducting research into bacteria. He happened to notice that a mold called penicillium had grown on a dish containing bacteria in his laboratory and had killed the germs. A few years later, a team of scientists led by Howard Florey, with backing from an American drug company, were able to produce sufficient quantities of penicillin to treat large numbers of soldiers wounded during World War II. Penicillin works on a wide range of bacteria.

During the early twentieth century, scientists searched for "magic bullets"—drugs to target a particular disease, or the germs that caused it, without otherwise harming the body. About 1910, German chemist Paul Ehrlich discovered the first (**magic bullet**.

In the 1920s Canadian scientists Frederick Banting (1891–1941) and Charles Best (1899–1978) discovered that insulin could control the high blood sugar levels in people with diabetes (an illness, caused by lack of insulin, in which the body cannot absorb sugar and starch properly). This discovery helped to ease the lives of millions of diabetics worldwide.

In 1928 chance led to another important breakthrough—the discovery of the germ-killing power of a mold (fungus) called *Penicillium*. In the early 1940s Howard Florey (1898–1968) and a group of British scientists isolated (**penicillin**,) the antibiotic (bacteria-killing substance) from the mold.

Whenever a new drug was discovered, scientists tested it carefully for harmful side effects before selling it commercially. In the 1950s tests failed to reveal the harmful effects of a drug named (**thalidomide**) until it was too late. After this tragedy, drugs had to pass even stricter tests.

World War II (1939–1945) brought changes. British surgeon Archibald McIndoe helped pioneer the technique of plastic surgery to treat soldiers who suffered from bad burns. During the war, sonar technology, which uses high-pitched sound waves to detect

Thalidomide

In the 1950s a German drug company developed a drug called thalidomide. It was used as a sleeping pill and to treat morning sickness during pregnancy. The drug had been on the market for just a short while when scientists discovered a major problem. Pregnant women who had taken the drug were giving birth to children with deformed limbs. Thalidomide was withdrawn immediately, but not before thousands of children with deformities were born worldwide. This tragedy led to even tighter controls for all new drugs.

A child with thalidomide deformities.

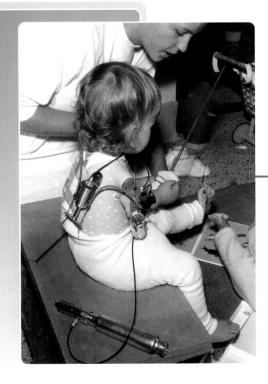

Kidney and Lung Machines

In the 1930s American surgeon John Gibbon invented the heart-lung machine, which took over from a patient's heart and lungs during major surgery. In the 1950s Dutch scientist Willem Kolff developed an "artificial kidney" or dialysis machine, which filtered the blood of patients whose kidneys had failed.

Heart–lung machines take over the jobs of the heart and lungs, which allows surgeons to carry out otherwise impossible operations in the chest.

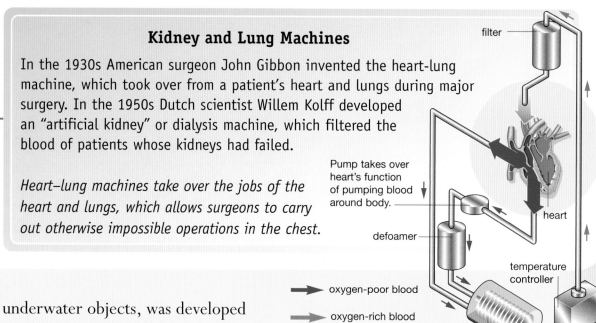

filter

Pump takes over heart's function of pumping blood around body.

heart

defoamer

temperature controller

→ oxygen-poor blood

→ oxygen-rich blood

Oxygenator takes over lung's role of adding oxygen to blood.

underwater objects, was developed to track submarines. Afterward, sonar gave rise to ultrasound, which uses sound waves to produce images of unborn babies in the womb.

Around the same time, scientists began to develop (machines) that could take over from major organs such as the lungs and kidneys. These made major surgery possible. They also paved the way for transplant surgery to replace damaged organs. Transplant operations often failed because patients' bodies rejected new organs, which contained "foreign" tissue. This led to the development of new drugs called immunosuppressants to suppress organ rejection. The first was cortisone, which was developed in the 1950s.

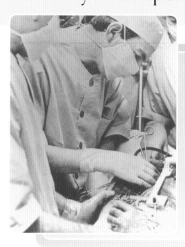

The First Heart Transplant

In 1967 Christiaan Barnard (1922–2001; left) transplanted the heart of a young woman who had died in a car crash into a 59-year-old man named Louis Washkansky. Washkansky survived for eighteen days before he died of pneumonia (the drugs he received to prevent rejection of his new heart also prevented his body from fighting the pneumonia). This pioneering operation paved the way for more successful heart operations.

In 1967, South African surgeon Christiaan Barnard carried out the first successful heart transplant. In the 1970s, the first liver, kidney, lung, and pancreas transplants followed. Soon doctors began to implant artificial body parts, including heart pacemakers to regulate heart rate, and even whole artificial hearts.

Inside every cell in our bodies, strands of DNA (deoxyribonucleic acid) contain the "blueprint of life"—coded instructions for all the inherited characteristics that parents pass on to their offspring. In 1953 two British scientists, Francis Crick (born 1916) and James Watson (born 1928), figured out the structure of DNA. Following this, in 1988, scientists around the world took part in the Human Genome Project, to map human genes. An initial draft map was completed in June 2000.

The Secret of DNA

In 1953 Watson and Crick discovered that the structure of DNA was a double helix—like a twisted ladder. The search to find DNA's structure had been a race between two teams of British scientists. The other team, made up of Maurice Wilkins (born 1916) and Rosalind Franklin (1920–1958), was also honored when Watson and Crick received the Nobel Prize for their work on DNA in 1962.

The rungs on the DNA ladder are made up of four chemicals called bases. A gene is several hundred or several thousand bases on a strand of DNA. DNA coils around itself to make chromosomes.

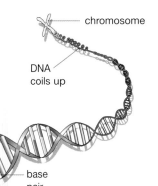

chromosome

DNA coils up

base pair

bases

7 | INTO THE FUTURE

The late twentieth century brought many new achievements in medicine, including new drugs and techniques for diagnosis and surgery. Rapid progress continues today.

IN THE LATE 1900S THE ARRIVAL of new (**scanning techniques**) made it easier for doctors to diagnose health problems. They included magnetic resonance imaging (MRI), which exploits the natural magnetism of certain atoms inside cells, and positron emission tomography (PET).

Instruments called (**endoscopes**) were invented in the 1830s. These long

New Scanners

PET and CT (computerized tomography) scanners are used to take images of cross sections or "slices" through the body. CT is a modern technique that combines X rays with computer technology to produce very detailed images.

A doctor examines the results from a scan.

Endoscopes—an Eye Inside the Body

Modern endoscopes not only carry light and a miniature camera, but also forceps or other tiny cutting tools such as scissors or tiny brushes to collect tissue samples. The light is carried down the long flexible tube by tiny glass strands (fiber optics). Endoscopes also supply water and air so surgeons can wash, dry, and inflate organs or tissues for a better view. Surgeons can carry out operations through small holes using endoscopes.

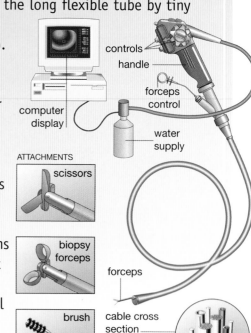

controls
handle
forceps control
water supply
computer display
ATTACHMENTS
scissors
biopsy forceps
forceps
brush
cable cross section
fiber-optic cable

tubes can be inserted into openings, such as the mouth, to see inside the body. Beginning in the 1950s the new technology of fiber optics allowed tiny cameras to be positioned at the end of fine endoscope tubes, which could then be inserted through small cuts in the skin. These instruments allowed surgeons to have a clear view of tissues and organs deep inside the body.

Starting in the 1980s, spare-part surgery, which enabled surgeons to replace many different body parts, advanced rapidly. At the same time, the new technique of keyhole surgery transformed many operations. Surgeons began to make only tiny cuts (keyholes) to perform simple operations such as removing the gall bladder. Endoscopes and lasers, which use a controlled beam

Spare-part Surgery

Many implants (artificial parts) repair or replace a part of the body that no longer works properly. Replacement parts include organs such as the eye, heart, liver, and kidney, and also blood vessels. There are also replacements for joints such as the knee, hip, and elbow joints, and even whole limbs. Implants containing radioactive materials can be inserted into tissue to treat cancers, and others containing drugs are inserted to release the drug over a long time. The diagram shows just some of the many body parts that can now be replaced by transplants from human donors or implants. Artificial parts are made of tough, durable materials such as steel and plastic.

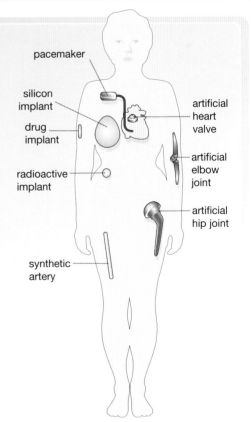

pacemaker

silicon implant

drug implant

radioactive implant

synthetic artery

artificial heart valve

artificial elbow joint

artificial hip joint

35

Space Medicine

In recent years a new branch of medicine has developed to tackle the special health problems faced by astronauts who spend time in space. In turn, space medicine has thrown light on some illnesses common on planet Earth.

Some of the health problems tackled by space medicine stem from the weightlessness astronauts experience away from the pull of gravity.

of pure light, now carry out almost bloodless operations from which patients recover very quickly.

In the twentieth century the arrival of space travel gave birth to a new branch of medical science: (**space medicine**.) Another development was worldwide vaccination programs to wipe out diseases that had been major killers. They included smallpox, eradicated in the 1970s. The poorest countries do not have the money to pay for vaccines. In these countries, diseases of poverty, such as cholera, kill many thousands of people each year.

In developed countries diseases such as cancer and heart disease remain major killers. A new science, epidemiology, has emerged to explore the reasons why diseases occur.

Genetic Engineering

In the course of the Human Genome Project, scientists tracked down the faulty genes that cause genetic (inherited) illnesses such as cystic fibrosis and hemophilia to pass from parents to children. In the near future the technique of genetic engineering, in which healthy new genes can be inserted into a person's DNA, may help scientists cure these diseases. Genetically engineered animals and other organisms will also help drug companies produce important drugs.

In the twenty-first century, scientists may succeed in finding a cure for cancer or for illnesses of the brain and nervous system, such as Alzheimer's and Parkinson's disease. Meanwhile, new strains of drug-resistant germs and even entirely new diseases appear. One deadly newcomer is **AIDS,** which attacks the body's immune system.

During the human genome project, scientists located the faulty **genes** that cause some hereditary illnesses to pass from parents to their children.

In the last thirty years there have been great advances in fertility treatment, which is helping couples who are unable to conceive naturally have children. It is impossible to predict what new breakthroughs will be made in medicine in the next fifty years or so, but it is certain that there will be many.

AIDS

In 1983 scientists tracked down the cause of AIDS (acquired immunodeficiency syndrome) to the HIV virus (right), which is transmitted from person to person in blood or through sexual contact. Drugs have now been developed to slow the progress of AIDS, but no one has yet found a cure. Another deadly newcomer, with flu-like symptoms, is the SARS virus, which spread to several countries in 2003.

HIV consists of strands of RNA, or ribonucleic acid. These carry the virus's "operating instructions," within a protein shell (capsid) and an outer envelope, also made of proteins.

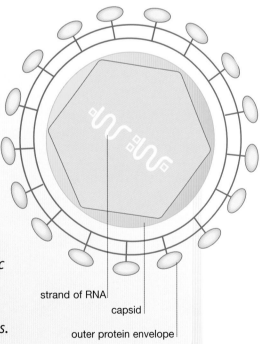

strand of RNA

capsid

outer protein envelope

Glossary

acupuncture A type of traditional Chinese medicine in which fine needles are inserted into the skin at key points on the body to cure illness.

anatomy The study of the body's structure.

anesthetic A drug that is given to numb the sensation of pain.

antibiotic A drug that cures bacterial infection.

antiseptic A chemical that kills bacteria.

aseptic Sterile, germ-free.

ayurveda A branch of medicine from India, which dates back more than three thousand years.

bacteria Simple organisms that are a major cause of disease, commonly called germs.

bile A fluid produced by the liver and stored in the gall bladder, which aids digestion.

cataract A health problem affecting the eye, in which the eye's lens becomes clouded. Surgeons can operate to remove a cataract.

cauterization An old-fashioned method of sealing wounds with heat, such as boiling oil.

chakra One of seven channels in the body through which energy flows, according to Indian medicine.

diagnosis The art of identifying illness.

disease An illness that can be caused by infection rather than injury.

dissect To cut up a plant or animal to examine its structure.

DNA A molecule containing the genetic (inherited) information that tells the body how to develop, which parents pass on to their offspring.

drug A chemical that is used to treat illness. Drugs can be either taken from living organisms or made chemically.

electrocardiograph (ECG) Instrument that records electrical activity in the heart.

electroencephalograph (EEG) Instrument that records electrical activity in the brain.

endoscope A long thin tube down which light can pass and which is inserted into an opening in the body or a small cut, so that doctors can see inner tissues or organs.

epidemic A widespread occurrence of a disease in a community at any one time.

gene A segment of DNA that carries the instructions to make one or several proteins. Genes control the inheritance of physical features from parent to offspring as well as the daily activities of body cells.

germ A general word for a variety of tiny organisms (living things) that can cause disease, including bacteria and viruses.

gland A body part which makes a substance, usually a liquid, that has a particular use.

magic bullet Drug that can target a particular disease, or the germs that cause it, without otherwise harming the body.

ophthalmoscope Instrument used to examine the eye.

organ A part of the body with a distinct function, such as the heart, liver, or eye.

panacea A remedy that will cure all illness.

pathology The medical study of disease.

plastic surgery Surgery to rebuild a damaged part of the body or improve a person's appearance.

prognosis The predicted course of a disease.

protist A primitive organism that can cause disease.

purging An old-fashioned technique for ridding the body of poison, sometimes by causing the patient to vomit or excrete.

side effect An unexpected and often undesirable effect of a drug on the body.

sphygmomanometer Instrument for measuring blood pressure.

spirometer An instrument to test a patient's lung capacity.

symptom A physical sign of illness, such as a high temperature or skin rash.

tissue A group of cells that all perform the same job, such as muscle tissue.

trepanning The ancient technique of drilling or cutting into the skull to relieve headache or rid the patient of evil spirits.

uroscopy The study of urine to diagnose illness.

vaccine A substance that triggers the body's immune system to defend itself against infection.

virus A microscopic particle that invades cells to reproduce, causing disease.

For More Information

BOOKS

Jeanne Bendick. *Galen and the Gateway to Medicine*. Bathgate, ND: Bethlehem Books, 2002.

Brandon Marie Miller. *Just What the Doctor Ordered: The History of American Medicine*. Minneapolis: Lerner Publications, 1997.

Jordan McMullin. *The Black Death*. Farmington Hills, MI: Greenhaven Press, 2003.

Steve Parker. *Eyewitness: Medicine*. New York: Dorling Kindersley, 2000.

Kathryn Senior and David Salariya. *You Wouldn't Want to be Sick in the Sixteenth Century! Diseases You'd Rather not Catch*. New York: Franklin Watts, 2002.

Brian R. Ward. *Eyewitness: Epidemic*. New York: Dorling Kindersley, 2000.

WEBSITES

BBC Education—Medicine Through Time
www.bbc.co.uk/education/medicine/
nonint/home.shtml
The history of medicine in the United Kingdom.

Brainpop Health
www.brainpop.com/
Colorful site featuring animated movies on health and medical matters.

Edward Jenner Museum
www.jennermuseum.com/overview/
index.shtml
All about Edward Jenner, the doctor who invented vaccination.

Kids' Health
www.kidshealth.org/kid/
All about childrens' health, including glossary of medical terms.

National Library of Medicine
www.nlm.nih.gov/hmd/hmd.html
The history of medicine, from Galen to recent medical advances.

A Science Odyssey: You Try It: A Doctor Over Time
www.pbs.org/wgbh/aso/tryit/doctor/
Find out how a doctor would have treated the same illness in 1900, 1950, and 1998.

Index